IN EVIDENCE

D0063251

UNIVERSITY OF PITTSBURGH PRESS

IN EVIDENCE

POEMS OF THE LIBERATION OF
NAZI CONCENTRATION CAMPS

BARBARA HELFGOTT HYETT

for Elie Wiesel

Published by the University of Pittsburgh Press,
Pittsburgh, Pa. 15260
Copyright © 1986, Barbara Helfgott Hyett
All rights reserved
Feffer and Simons, Inc., London
Manufactured in the United States of America

Library of Congress Cataloging in Publication Data

Helfgott Hyett, Barbara.
  In evidence.

  1. World War, 1939–1945—Poetry. 2. Concentration
camps—Poetry. 3. Holocaust, Jewish (1939–1945)—
Poetry. I. Title.
PS3558.E4744I5 1986   811'.54   85-22574
ISBN 0-8229-3526-0
ISBN 0-8229-5376-5 (pbk.)

The author wishes to thank the following institutions for
permission to quote from archives of liberators' testimony:
Boston University Hillel Foundation, "Liberators Remember:
An Oral History Archive"; The Center for Holocaust Studies,
Documentation and Research, Brooklyn College, Brooklyn,
New York; The Oral History Office, Department of His-
tory, Northeastern University, Boston, Massachusetts; The
United States Holocaust Memorial Council, Washington,
D.C.; and Johns Hopkins University Press for permission to
quote from *The Papers of Dwight David Eisenhower: The
War Years,* edited by Alfred D. Chandler, Jr.

Some of these poems have previously appeared in *The Croton
Review, Genesis 2,* and *Martyrdom and Resistance.*

CONTENTS

ACKNOWLEDGMENTS

I am grateful to the Arts Council of Brookline, Massachusetts, and the Artists Fellowship Award program of the Massachusetts Council on the Arts and Humanities for grants which partially funded this project; to Temple Ohabei Shalom, Brookline, Massachusetts, for the generous contribution of office space; to the members of "Project Liberators Remember," particularly Barbara Abromovitz and Alan Rosen; to Jean Lunn for her meticulous copy editing and Pat Aristegui for her typing; to Kathi Aguero, Carol Dine, Martha Hauptman, Tom Hurley, Mary Rosen, Judy Rosenberg, Paula Sirois, and Beverly Smith who have contributed time and expertise toward the completion of this manuscript; and especially to my husband, Norman, and our sons, Eric Emanuel and Brian Helfgott Hyett for their faith in this work, and for their support.

PREFACE

Forty-one years ago, in July, the liberation of the Nazi concentration camps began. The Soviet army had captured Lublin, and Majdanek was set free. The end of the war was in sight. But annihilation continued at the death camps. Between May and November, 1944, one-half million Hungarian and Slovakian Jews were gassed. By January, 1945, the Allies had reached the Rhine, and the Soviets liberated Auschwitz from which, only days before, the prisoners who could walk were marched away and shipped in freight cars to other German camps.

That same winter, partisans and members of the camp underground liberated slave labor and concentration camps in a sweep across the continent from Russia and the Balkan States as far west as France. On April 4, the Fourth Armored Division of the American Third Army liberated Ohrdruf and, a week later, another unit took Buchenwald. On April 15, British Army and Canadian units liberated Bergen-Belsen and established a hospital there. But the liberators were too late. Thousands who lived to be set free died of typhus and starvation in the weeks after liberation. As the Allied Forces closed in, they liberated Flossenbürg, Landsberg, Oranienburg, Ebensee, Mauthausen and other satellite camps in Germany and Austria.

And still the mass murders continued. At Gardelegen, the day before it was liberated, the SS locked the inmates in a barn and burned them alive. On April 19, the 222nd U.S. Infantry, the 42nd Rainbow Division, liberated Dachau. Nazi Germany unconditionally surrendered on May 7, 1945, but the last concentration camp, Theresienstadt, was not fully liberated for another few days.

In spite of what preparation their soldiering might have provided, those who entered the camps could not believe what they saw there. On April 20, General Eisenhower, Commander in Chief of the Allied forces, sent the following cable to General Marshall:

We continue to uncover German concentration camps for political prisoners in which conditions of indescribable horror prevail. I have visited one of these myself and I assure you that whatever has been printed on them to date has been understatement.

—from *The Papers of Dwight David Eisenhower: The War Years,* edited by Alfred D. Chandler, Jr.

Years later, the liberators would be both reluctant and compelled to tell what they had seen, what they had done.

★

In the fall of 1980, a group of volunteers gathered for the purpose of conducting interviews with American liberators. The work became an oral history archive, conceived by Rabbi Joseph Polak, himself a survivor of the camps, who now serves as director of B'nai B'rith Hillel at Boston University.

The project team included a psychiatrist, a psychiatric nurse, social workers, an Israeli engineer, a poet, professors, and graduate and undergraduate students in history, psychology, and theology. It was our task to gather tapes, photographs, and supporting documents that testify to the conditions in the camps as witnessed by the liberators. We studied history, from the Third Reich's program for the elimination of the Jewish people to the military tactics of the liberation. We established interviewing procedures and tech-

niques for dealing with the sensitive testimony
we were to receive.

Then we solicited veterans by advertising in
newspapers in the Greater Boston area, and con-
ducted thirty-seven interviews in the partici-
pants' homes from May 1981 through August 1984.
In most cases, the veterans were giving this tes-
timony for the first time. My role was to devise
questions to probe their silence and their pain.
(The tapes, photographs, and memorabilia are
housed in the Hillel Library at Boston Univer-
sity and plans are being made to establish libera-
tor archives in public libraries in surrounding
communities.) In addition to these interviews,
I read transcripts from similar oral history proj-
ects at Brooklyn College, Emory University, and
Northeastern University.

Two years after the first interview, I began the
poems about the liberation. At first, I tried to
write as a child on the train to Dachau, but I
could not speak for the victims. Then, I wrote
as an observer, but these poems were faceless.
So I listened to all the tapes again, and this time
heard the music in the words. I selected details
from the accounts, maintaining the language as
it was spoken, changing very few words, and
then only for the sake of clarity. I arranged the
poems to create a narrative sequence, imagining
a voice—a young soldier who is there, watching,
not necessarily comprehending, letting the hor-
ror wash over him.

Later, when I showed the manuscript to three
of the liberators I had interviewed, and thanked
them for the poems, each one told me not to
thank him, that the poems were mine. Now I
wonder: whose responsibility is it to document
history? I did not write these poems, I found

them. I see this work as an interaction between the liberators, who told their experiences, and the poet who heard them. I offer these poems in an effort to redeem memory, to gather something from the humanity of the GIs who liberated the camps, and who wept openly at what they found.

Barbara Helfgott Hyett
Boston
April 1985
Nisan 5745

SPRING, 1945

I'm sitting in
my jeep someplace,
listening to
the radio and
the commentator
is saying, *There
are just a few
skirmishes now.
The war is about
to end,* when
another jeep
goes by with a
young boy on it,
most of his
stomach blown
away. He was
still alive. I
could tell.

❖

You have to believe
you have a chance
to stay alive. You
don't know who the hell
you're firing at, unless
you're a marksman. I
was never a hero. If
there was someplace I
could hide for a while,
without getting anybody
hurt, that was where
I'd go. I'd peek now
and then. I'd probably
pull the trigger. But
I didn't know whether
I was shooting at a
tree, or the ground,
or a bird.

*E*ven though it was war,
Germany was a beautiful
place. I could look out
my window and see the Tyrol
in the morning when the sun
hit it, the golden snow.
You see the death camp. You
see the snowy mountain,
brooks running down the
sides of it, the stones,
the green valley, shells
landing right in the middle
of it.

✦

*T*here was a canister
explosion — hundreds
of ball bearings and
pieces of steel flying
everywhere. I hid in
a ditch in the field.
I hit my elbow on a
rock. *Oh Holy Christ.*
I'm screaming. A medic
happened to be behind
me, and I'm saying,
*I'm hit. My arm is
broken.* So he pulled
up my sleeve and said,
*What do you want,
A Purple Heart?*
I said, *Yeah.*
And they gave me one.

I was walking past
a railyard that the
Royal Air Force bombers
had torn apart, engines
lying over on their side,
cars standing on end.
Acres of railyard torn
to shreds, and there
was an old German woman,
seventy-five, eighty
years old walking down
the street, carrying an
umbrella, and when she
passed me, she hit me
with her umbrella and
she said, in perfect
English, *Who'd you hit?*
I laughed and I said,
Lady, I didn't mean it.

◆

*T*he major was
an accountant
for the Ford
Motor Company.
He was in his
late forties,
in the infantry
and he wasn't
qualified for
the infantry
any longer.
He was not
the combat type.
He had lived
a lifetime of
accountability.

My friend Mo Greenberg
pitched a tent
outside homes
all across Europe,
the only American
soldier living
in a tent. Every
other fellow in
our battalion
was inside a nice
fortress, a home.
But Mo was outside
in a tent. He
refused to displace
civilians, German
civilians, even
though they had
persecuted his race.

◆

We were American
POWs and we
had our times
on the road. We
had our times in
camp. Every
morning we had
eggs and toast
and coffee. The
Germans never
mistreated
their prisoners.
When we heard about
the concentration
camps we couldn't
believe it. I
guess they didn't
hate us the way
they hated the Jews.

*A*fter I was shot down
over Czechoslovakia,
I was interrogated
at a camp where
every window was
shuttered. Inside,
the Gestapo, strange
breed of man. And
other men, dressed
in old prison
uniforms, stripes,
and they were barefoot.
Every time the German
interrogator snapped
his fingers, like
that, a man would
bow his head. So
obsequious, *Yes, sir,
no, sir.* The place
was loaded with these
prisoners. Poor
little old men.

You understand, I was mad
during the whole war. I
hadn't expected quite what
I was seeing. After all,
you don't expect things
you can't imagine. You
focus your anger. My enemy
was the German. It was all
very simple for me. There
was an enemy I knew how I
felt about. I was really
mad all the time.

OPENING THE GATES

A shock wave ran through
everyone and the ones who
hit it first passed the word
to the others coming up
in back. *You know:*
what you're going to see,
you're not going to believe.

✦

*I*n our battalion
every man had
a place to ride.
The guns were
pulled by trucks.
I had access to
a small car. We
were issued maps.
Each of us had
a map showing where
Dachau was. It was
just another sally
down the road.

*W*hat they had was a moat
that must have been filled
with water because in order
to get into the camp we
had to go across a bridge.
That bridge is very vivid,
the entrance and the exit
of hell.

❖

As we rolled over
the bridge, I looked
at the water going
underneath and I
thought to myself,
I don't understand
why we should
continue living
if the human race
does not consider
itself above the
animals.

I rode into Dachau
on a jeep, over a
very narrow bridge.
It was a clear day,
a very clear day,
the kind of weather
where you'd need a
jacket. We'd just
finished a winter of
sleeping in encampments,
so any sunshine was
welcome. We crossed a
bridge and the first
thing I saw were piles
of shoes, all kinds of
shoes, a pyramid of shoes.

✦

A wagon with rubber tires,
wheels, the size of a car,
a freight car, a train,
bodies stacked inside and
heaping, one of the sides
dropped down so you could
see the pile of bodies.
I counted eighty bodies
stacked three feet high
like a haystack.

*A*nd there was a train,
a passenger train made
up of the oldest
railroad cars I have
ever seen. They must
have dated from the
Franco-Prussian war.
Old cars, the kind with
compartments, each of
which had its own set
of doors, like so many
stagecoaches set together.
The most ghastly thing
about the cars was that
they were fully occupied
by dead people sitting
upright in their seats.

◆

When we came upon
the train with
all the bodies,
our general gave
an order that, from
every company, two
soldiers would be
brought there to see.
He wanted his soldiers
to go back and tell
their buddies what
had happened there.

*E*ight freight cars,
doors nailed shut,
big slabs of boards
across the doors,
and the American
soldiers had pried
most of them loose.
The bodies jammed in.
Doors nailed shut.
They must have been on
that siding for days
in the heat of the sun,
urinating, defecating
where they stood. Many
of them dead for days.

◆

*I*n those stinking cars
I saw the bodies
of prisoners too weak
to get out. A few
tried and they made
a bloody heap in the
door, machine-gunned
by the SS. A little
girl was in that car.

In one car, sitting
on the bodies of
his comrades, his
face contorted with
pain frozen by death,
was the body of one
who'd completed the
amputation of his
gangrenous leg with
his own hands. The
stump was covered with
paper. Close by, one
who'd been beaten
until his entrails
protruded from his
back. But most of
them had simply died
in the attitude of
absolute exhaustion
that only starving
men can assume.

◆

I got physically
sick at the
freight cars.
The stench of
flesh, the
waste that
they were
caked with.
I got sick.
A lot of us
got sick.
The prisoners
themselves,
inside the
camp, didn't
get sick.
In fact,
at the time
I wondered
if they
thought we
were sissies.

It was a warm summer day,
flies buzzing all over
the bodies decomposing on
the siding, partway through
the gates. We knew the camp
was just beyond the large
arched wall, red bricks, a
chain link fence. I'll never
get the stench out of my nose.
*Retribution is mine, saith
the Lord.*

◆

Compassion
doesn't come
immediately.
First, disbelief.
You don't believe.
You don't want to
believe. You're so
boggled. It's only
later that you feel
compassion. First
the mind has to
recognize what's going on.

◆

We had orders to extend
as much compassion as
possible, but as soon
as they saw the trains,
our men became animals.
Their minds had changed.
Nothing could keep them
from shooting. Nothing.

✦

*W*e met no
resistance.
We could
have sent
a small
penetrating
group in if
we had any
idea that
there'd be
no resistance.
We attacked
with a full
battalion,
everything
that was not
needed.

*W*e came in twenty
trucks, full of
infantrymen.
We made a big
circle in the
parade ground.
My duty was to
protect the truck
from the prisoners.
We had to keep them
away from our food.
For the next half
hour, my job was to
stand there with a
rifle, a bayonet
attached, and keep
these people away.

✦

*T*aking things away
from people, that was
our job. We had been
trained. We were all
soldiers. Our first job
was to kill.

We used to just
sort of straddle
the back of the
halftrack and I
remember riding
on there and
these people came
and tried to kiss
my feet and I
didn't want them
kissing my feet.
It didn't seem right
for human beings
to be kissing other
human beings' feet.

◆

I was alone
guarding my side
of the truck and
this old man,
probably no older
than I am now,
said something and
pointed to the food
and kept making
motions that he
wanted to put
food in his mouth.
There were a lot
of candy bars
spread on the edge
of the truck and he
begged for them. I
kept pushing him
away, *No. No. Go
away.* And he went
down on his knees
in front of me and
looked up, begging
from me, kneeling
before me. It was
hard not to give
him what he wanted.

*W*e were told we were
going up to a camp
of political prisoners.
They were going to be
deloused. We were told
not to get too close.
But when we actually
got there, I thought
it was an insane asylum.

◆

*A*s we drove into
the camp, a pound
of butter fell off
one of our trucks
and these human
beings fell on it
like a pack of wild
dogs. And I'm all
of nineteen years
old, seeing this.

I was one of the few
Jews in my outfit, the
20th Armored Division,
Southern Division, mostly
Okies, swamp runners,
Floriders and hillbillies,
whatever name you want to
call them. I don't think
there were six Jews in
the whole division. I
took my lumps for being
Jewish. I got beat up
more times than I played
cards on Saturday night.
And when I saw the camps,
I wanted to march the whole
goddamn world through so
they'd believe that this
had happened. I wanted
all those bastards to see.

◆

I was right there
when the gates
swung open and
those poor things
came stumbling out.
They fell out like
flies and they died
right in front of me,
but we were forced
back into our truck
and we were not
allowed to touch
them because they
were diseased.
Some of them just
dropped right in
front of us and we
were helpless. We
had to stay in the truck.

I'm not well educated.
I could never
describe what
I saw there.
There is no
film that could
describe the
sight. Even
if it was filmed
in 3-D you could
never describe it.

The first thought
I had was: if we
had known this
two years before
now the goddamn
war would have
been over
in six months.
Jesus Christ.
If we had known.

THE PRISONERS

Our men cried.
We were a
combat unit.
We'd been to
Anzio, to
southern France,
Sicily, Salerno,
the Battle of
the Bulge, and
we'd never, ever
seen anything
like this.

*W*e walked into
a wooden barn
with people
stretched out
on either side,
people lying
on straw and
burlap bags,
a sour, putrid
smell that
left you ready
to throw up.
They wore coats
over the stripes.
I don't remember
how cold it was.

*T*heir clothes were rags. Some had crude shoes with wooden soles. Some had rags wrapped around their feet. Most of them were barefooted.

◆

How do they keep themselves
upright, the bone showing
right through the flesh, the
translucent veins? You can
almost see blood going through
the ears, the lips, the nose,
the eyes deep sunken, burning,
terrible.

*T*oo weak to stand, they lay
on straw under heavy blankets,
skin stretched so taut
over joints they couldn't
bend their arms.
When we passed by they
cowered against the wall,
turned their faces
from the expected blow.

◆

I yelled *Christ,*
get a medic. Get
something. Some
of these people
are still alive.
It was pathetic.
Their eyes were
pleading but they
couldn't talk. And
you couldn't do
anything for them
because they were
all shrunk up.

I never have seen
anybody so emaciated,
just literally
skeletons, you know,
breathing skeletons.
I used to ask myself,
Is this a man or
a woman I'm speaking to?

◆

In some of the bunks, the men
didn't beat on their tins
at all and just lay still.
Some of their eyes were open
and that was terrible
and some of their eyes were
closed and that was worse.

*T*here is an artist
who draws children
with large eyes—
I forget her name.
If you take those
eyes and put hell
in them, those
large eyes, even
in the smallest
face, this is
what you're looking
into at the camps.

◆

*T*hey'd approach us
for cigarettes,
candy, to try
to establish
a connection.
We were afraid
they'd want us
to get them out
of the camp. As
a soldier, there's
very little you
can do. So you
try to avoid an
entanglement. You
just don't promise
anybody anything.

We were afraid
to get near
them. They were
like lepers.
Poor people. We
had compassion.
We were prisoners
in another sense.
I'd been drafted.
Do you think for
one minute, if
any of us had
a choice, we'd
be there? We'd
be back home, safe,
playing ball.

✦

In the Jewish section
there were these
individuals who were
cowering to one side
and the Jewish leader
approached us, asking
permission to kill them.
They were prisoners
themselves but they
were Christian—a very
subtle type of punishment
for Christians to be
put in the Jewish section.
These three had turned
into guards, *Kapos,*
and now the Jewish person
wanted permission to kill
them. I grew up a farm
boy in North Dakota. Why
was this guy asking me
to act like God? My
friend who was with me
answered him: *No.*
Absolutely not. There's
been enough killing.

Black bread, dark bread,
all kinds of bread, wagons
heaped with loaves of bread.
And when we tried to give
this man a loaf and that man
a loaf and let them divide
it, there was no such thing.
They tore at it like animals.

◆

*H*uman beings. These
are human beings. No cheeks.
No muscles in the chin. Only
skin and lips like paper tapes,
men thrashing like animals
but less graceful, begging—
But your clean American hands
don't want to touch them,
alive with lice. Stinking.
Still, you have to. So you think
of the twenty thousand others
for whom things have to be done
and before you can lift a finger
another thousand are dead and you
don't feel anything except
Jesus Christ Jesus Christ Jesus Christ.

We asked them for names
of their relatives in the
United States. You know,
when someone is in that
state, you grasp at straws.
Imagine someone saying, *Yeah,*
I have somebody who lives
in New York. A relative.
His name is Sam Cohen. We ask,
Well, where does he live?
and he says, *New York. You'll*
find him. He's in New York.
Sam Cohen. You'll find him.

✦

A prisoner gave me a boat
he'd taken from the house
of Ilse Koch. Ilse Koch,
the beast of Buchenwald.
It was a sailboat. *Santa
Maria*, the Madonna painted
in gilt, the child in gilt,
three painted crosses, a boat
with sails of human skin.

◆

One man wanted to
show us how thin
he was and how
they had abused
him. Another
showed us the
tattoo, numbers
on his hand.
They were mostly
in a fog. They
were no longer
prisoners, but
it just took time
for that to sink in.

◆

*H*e asked me for cigarettes.
I had a package in my pocket.
I think there were seven cigarettes
and I gave him the package. I said,
Divide this among your men
and I made a motion so that he
understood that I wanted him to
share those but he took them
and dumped them all in his pocket
and the other men saw it.

*O*ne prisoner
told me there
was a Greek
there. I
speak Greek
fluently.
I'm sorry I
didn't have
the occasion
to find a
Greek in Dachau.

✦

Whatever we had we gave freely:
some cheese, a can of beef.
I gave all my cigarettes away.
I couldn't speak to them but
in signs. We were glad that
they were free, that they didn't
have to worry anymore.

I was the chaplain's assistant
and when the captain, a rabbi
from Providence, Rhode Island,
spoke to them, in Yiddish, *Ich
bin ahn Americana rov,* all
of the emotions were unleashed.
There was wailing as if it were
Yom Kippur in an old-fashioned
town, the only Orthodox shul.
The people came over to us and
kissed our hands, and our boots.

◆

When we met the inmates,
we told them that we
were Jewish soldiers,
and when we were telling
them, we were talking
with tears, the biggest
tears you've ever seen.

*I*n the children's cell block,
the bedding, the clothing,
the floors besmeared with
months of dysentery, I could
put my fingers around their
upper arms, their ankles,
so little flesh. Two hundred
and fifty children. Children
of prisoners. Polish children.
Czechoslovakian children. I
can't remember what I did
after I saw the children.

*A*t the hospital we were greeted by a Dutch doctor who had been told earlier in the day that he was going to die that night. We told him that he was liberated now, and that the fear he had been living with for five years was to be forgotten.

We really didn't camp.
We didn't go to bed.
It was that struggle
to keep people alive.
We gave blood, whole
blood, got oxygen
into them that way.
The first day, three
thousand died. The
third day we were
there, we lost two.
It was a minor miracle.

✦

I used to speak of
the bodies as *stiffs.*
They weren't human,
they were objects.
This was not life.
If I tried the more
humane approach, I
couldn't get by.

*M*y task was separating
the living from the dead.
I had to go from stretcher
to stretcher with my
stethoscope and if there
was a person alive I had
to tell the soldiers, and
if I thought a person was
not alive, I sent him to
the mortuary and I remember
once, when I walked into
the mortuary, the person
that I thought was dead
sat up. I was more careful
after that.

◆

That afternoon, I gave
about twenty-five
injections. Trying to
get into these patients'
veins is really a job.
They are so thin. My
hand fits easily around
their upper arms.

We tried to coax
some of the prisoners
out of the barracks,
a couple of GIs
saying, *It's all right,
come on out.* But they
were afraid to come out.
I guess they thought
they were going to be
shot.

◆

I had a dog with me.
He'd been with me
throughout the war—
a Chesapeake retriever.
Now, the Nazis used to
torment people, used to
tear them apart with
German shepherd dogs.
So, when I walked in,
everybody was afraid.

*D*ead men. I think
everybody has seen
them, seen entrails,
seen buddies blown
apart, shredded by
mortar and artillery.
But a soldier had a
chance. People in
the line had a chance.
They were up front
when they were killed.
But people in the camp
had no chance. They
had to go. There was
no way they could fight.

◆

The smell was mingled death
and disinfectant, the hallways
jammed, straw pallets, beds
where skeletons lay curled.
On the top floor, one or two
could talk. We handed out
cigarettes. Some lay
staring right through you
with eyes that were sunk
actually halfway into
their heads. Some cried
continually. Some groaned.
Some could smile. Outside,
many lay in the sun near
a huge fire, under blankets,
shivering, though we
were hot in our GI clothes.

Wedding rings, lockets,
actual fillings from
people's teeth.
The lockers.
The filing cabinets
full of baby shoes.
The hair.
I cannot say *I understand.*
I did not see the lampshades.

ASHES

*T*he barracks had
no sides. It was
open to the air,
just a roofed-over
area and, oh, it
was big. There
were three tiers
of beds, wooden
boxes. We were so
repulsed by the
whole thing that
we couldn't go
in. Your heart
ached for what you
saw, but you didn't
want to touch,
didn't want to
get too near.

◆

Cedar posts
sunk in the
ground with
barbed wire
and bough
branches, pine
boughs and
barbed wire,
the beds of
these people.

*T*he bunks were logs
and I don't mean
logs with the bark off.
They were just logs like
you take off the ground
and that's what they
were sleeping on.
And there were turnips
on the floor. They were
very dark.

◆

At the end of the room,
one toilet. One toilet
for a thousand people.
And at the other end,
a door, a drop to
the wheelbarrow for
the bodies that didn't
get up in the morning.
Next door was the
doctor's office where,
if you went in, you were
dead when you came out.

And I went in
to take a picture
and the stench was so much
I couldn't. Now Joe,
who was with me, who
had been a fireman in
New York, stayed
a little bit longer.
But I couldn't
stay in line
to take the picture
so I went outside
and took a picture
of the building.

✦

We were shown the special
barracks for the women.
I don't know who they were.
Probably Jewish women.
Probably Yugoslav women.
I didn't see one black
person in the camp. This
was a brothel for German
officers in the camp.

*I*t was bleak and
very stark. They
had a big sign in
the front which
said, in German:
*If you work, you
become free.* It
was a delusion.
The main intent
of the camp was
to kill. And it
wasn't done in
a kind manner.
It was degrading.
They killed them
one piece at a time.

◆

The gas chamber
was nothing
more than an
empty shell.
The soldier
who accompanied
us had to point
out the nozzles.

When we saw
the ovens,
we were
silent.
Not a word
spoken, not
a single
expression.
Not, *Oh Jesus,*
not, *What is
this?* Not,
*What have we
done?*

◆

The cookery was a
concrete building
about the size of
an average home
and in the walls
there were fans
so that the air
would blow in,
half fans, so
that the screams
would not blow out.

◆

*T*he crematory was divided
into three sections and
the center section housed
the four huge ovens. In
each oven there were eight
bodies, and the ashes of
the bodies were divided
into eight separate parts
and placed into eight tin
cans, a name written on
each. One out of a hundred
turned out to be the ashes
of the person named, while
the rest were ashes with
the wrong name on the can.

◆

*T*he ovens were
in the middle and
around the wall
were grappling
hooks such as
you see in
butcher shops.
And two or
three feet below
the hooks, etched
into the concrete
of the building,
scratch marks of
the fingernails
of the people
who had been hanged
there alive, people
waiting their turn
in their anguish.

◆

And there were
bones. God,
there were bones, all
over the place,
wherever you
looked, like
pebbles,
wherever you
stepped there
were little
bits of bones.

◆

Near the crem023, I
remember stooping down
and picking up a piece
of something black: I
realized it was a bone.
I was going to throw it
down again. I thought,
*My God. This may be all
that's left of someone.*
So I wrapped it up in
my handkerchief and
carried it with me. It was
a couple of days later
that I dug it out of my
pocket. And I buried it.

At Buchenwald, they
put the bones of
individuals into
black boxes with
their numbers, or
even their names
on them. There were
piles of these
boxes. You could
fill rooms with
them. And all of
them were broken.
The inmates would
climb upon the piles,
searching through,
looking for numbers
or a name. All they'd
do was look.
Numbers and names.
They'd hold up
a box. And then
they'd put it down.

◆

Just outside
the crematorium
there was a huge
pile of ash.
Just think how
many bodies that
comprised. And
there was an
enormous wagon,
a hay wagon, sixty
bodies without
one ounce of flesh,
sixty bodies
ready to burn.

Ashes were still
in the room,
and in the far
corner, hanging
above the ovens,
a poem by Goethe,
in German, a poem
about the beauty
of death by fire.

◆

The final solution:
they wanted to
exterminate
the Jews to have
a pure race.
Definitely. It
was definitely
the Jews. It
was directed at
the Jews. They
annihilated
six million
Jews. God knows
the actual count.
Nobody knows
the count.

Any evidence
that would be
incriminating
to the Nazis
was not to be
disturbed.
Bodies weren't
to be moved
if they were
outside the
ovens and if
they were in
the ovens,
they were not
to be moved.

◆

The ovens,
the stench,
I couldn't repeat
the stench. You
have to breathe.
You can wipe out
what you don't want
to see. Close your
eyes. You don't want
to hear, don't want
to taste. You can
block out all senses
except smell.

You know, the funny thing is
the memories I have—
I'm not sure that I could say
where I was, what I was doing.
The only thing I have
is the picture that I know
I took. I took the picture.
I had the camera. I had to
have been there. Otherwise
I wouldn't have known.

THE GUARDS

Our captain told us
that there were SS
guards still in the
camp, hidden there
in inmates' clothing,
and that the prisoners
themselves would take
care of them. We were
not to interfere with
camp justice.

✦

    *W*e didn't know who
were the prisoners,
who the criminals,
who might be Germans
in disguise. Our job
was to keep them in.
We became the new
guards who stayed outside
the electrified fence.

I didn't see a guard
that I considered to
be of military age—
none between fifteen
and fifty. They were
all old men, or kids.

◆

At my guardpost,
there was a latrine,
an open ditch. One
day these people
came. They did not
look like scarecrows.
They were Poles, not
Jews. They brought
a man and threw him
into the latrine.
Then they jumped down
in there with him
and stomped on him
with their heels.

One night, walking
along the electric
fence, I saw the
naked body of a
man strung into
the barbed wire,
his hands pushed
through the fence.
I don't know how
they killed him.
There were no
physical signs.
He wasn't a normal
prisoner. He had
meat on his bones.
He'd miscalculated.
He didn't get out
of the camp soon
enough.

◆

I saw them dismember people.
I saw them string them up
against the wall. Not our
soldiers, but the inmates.
A group of them pulling
a man apart, our soldiers
looking the other way.

*W*e had caught two
guards and were
holding them in
the guardhouse,
a jail with two
cells. Sometime
during the night,
a third guard was
captured by the
prisoners and they
decapitated him.
They put his head
into a box and came
into the guardhouse
and put the box in
with the guards to
show them. And all
of us went in to
look because this
was an historical
thing that was
happening.

✦

*A*s we left
the place, we
saw a number
of inmates in
their striped
pajamas beating
a man with
sticks, heavy
sticks they
must have
found. An SS
guard they'd
identified.
He'd gotten
into civilian
clothes and was
trying to get
away. You know,
the major and I
talked about
this for months
afterwards.
We tried to
understand
ourselves. We
sat there and
watched them
beat him to
death. We
didn't lift
a finger.

*T*hey had taken an SS
prisoner. The roles
were reversed. They
had a German prisoner.
The only weapons they
used were bare palms.
They killed him with
their hands. We
watched that. We
wouldn't interfere.
We didn't know which
way was which. Three
of us. Sixty of them.
So we backed off.

◆

Just before we packed up,
two prisoners who'd been
out in the woods, very
young prisoners, two
German soldiers walked
into the camp. I guess
they'd been hiding. They
gave themselves up
to a corporal. They looked
pitifully alone.

I don't know that
we were angry.
We were too numb
for that. We were
drained, iced over,
frozen. It was
just too much. We
couldn't take it
in. We couldn't
have any human
feelings. That
came later, when
I woke for a month
of nights, screaming.

THE WAY BACK

And there were pits,
I would say about fifty
yards long, and people
buried alive in there.
And they had German
civilians digging them
out—but they wouldn't
touch the bodies—with
shovels. Two at a time.
You could see that the
bodies were still warm.
The soldiers, the infantry
men were so angered by
what they had seen that
they made the civilians
throw the shovels away
and take them out by hand
and lay them gently down.

*T*he first mass
of bodies was
done away with
by bulldozers,
unceremoniously.
And the prisoners
just kept dying.
We were burying
a hundred people
a day, using as
laborers the people
of the city of Linz.
Each morning, a truck
went in, looking
for important-
looking men: dentists,
doctors, insurance
agents, anybody
dressed up with
a briefcase. And
all day long these
men would bury the
dead, digging their
graves, carrying
them over, one
at a time.

*T*he next day
they brought
in some army
trucks, two
or three loads
of high-ranking
German officers
and they took
them down to
the barracks and
made them walk
through there,
and the Germans
kept saying:
verstehe nicht,
verstehe nicht.
I don't understand.
Ich verstehe nicht.

◆

We could never
understand the
townspeople not
knowing about
the camps. They
swore they never
knew. They told
us there were
camps in the
United States.
But there was
no way you couldn't
know. No matter
which way the wind
blew, you could
smell it.

Outside the camp, before
you cross the bridge,
there's a peaceful little
community. Later, when
we asked the people of
Dachau, *Didn't you know?*
Couldn't you tell from
the stench? they said
No. In German. We spoke
our best Yiddish and they
answered *No.*

✦

There was a small farm
right outside the camp
where potatoes were
growing. The prisoners
would sneak out, these
skinny bodies would
sneak through the wire.
They'd run into the farm
and, with their hands,
dig up a few potatoes.
Then they'd run back in.
Our officers told us to
put a stop to it. To
shoot them. But I don't
know anybody who did.

*T*hey were very bitter
people, angry as hell
and they thought they
were entitled—as
they were—to get
what they could get
their hands on: food,
clothes, things like
that. They were already
looting, ganging up on
Germans if they could
find them. One or two
crying in a feeble way.
A lot of hand shaking,
hand wringing, all these
people wandering in the
streets. They were also
in the way. I mean,
they were in the way, see?

*H*ere these people are
finally liberated. They're
waiting to find their
families. They're waiting
to leave these camps and we
can't let them, for fear
of the German population
hurting them, or for the sake
of law and order. So they're
kept in camps. Detention
camps. Who's going to be
happy with that, and what's
my lot now?

These prisoners, these laboring folk
had busted out of Erfurt, a small
town, a big highway, and they were
roaming, pillaging the countryside.
Our instructions were to go in there
and shove them back in their place.
Three of us went in. There must have
been two thousand people, all of them
men, and we were the enemy, making
them stay in or be shot. My sympathies
were with them. I didn't care if they
tore up the whole country. That's what
I thought we were there to do anyway.

✦

As much as we tried
to keep the camps
closed until they
were processed so
they'd know who
they were, where
they came from,
which country,
which family—
we tried to keep
them together but
they did get away.

We were on our way
back, but there
were other soldiers
still on their way
to the front and
they would say,
*Hey, you think you
had it tough? You
oughta see the camps
we just liberated.*
We said, *you oughta
see the forest out
there and the flies
the bulldozers are
pushing off the bodies.*

✦

In the hedgerows
I noticed a set
of dogtags and
a bloodstained
helmet from the
Second Division.
I had just been
to Buchenwald.
What was I to do?
I buried them
on the spot where
I'd found them
and I said
the Kaddish there,
in the evening,
with God
as my minyan.

*O*ur general
was a very good man.
In Austria, at the camp
for displaced persons,
he told me: *Let's*
make a list of what
we need to make life
more livable for the
Jews. Soap. Things
like that. So I drew
up a list. The general
called in the supply
officer and said:
Get these things. But
the soldier said,
General, how can I?
The economy of Austria
had collapsed. Where
am I going to get these
things? And the general
said: *I said, get it.*
and he said, *Yes, SIR.*

◆

*I*n Salzburg, I met
a lot of the people
who'd been liberated.
They were on their way
out of the sphere
of German influence,
going through the Alps,
a railroad tunnel into
Italy, where they could
take a boat, possibly,
to Israel.

*I*n the town,
the factory
employed some
Hungarian
Jewish girls.
And they were
starving. We
got them some
potatoes and
some onions
and a bolt of
cloth and they
made dresses.
They were all
wearing the same
dress out of
the same cloth.
And I took a
picture of them
and they signed
it in Yiddish:
*Thank you from
the Hungarian
Jewish girls.*

A prisoner of war told me
that he had been in the
Boy Scouts. His greatest
love was Buffalo Bill. He
played cowboys and Indians,
same as we did, only in
German. Until Hitler. Then
the Boy Scouts changed.

In Wörgl, in Austria,
the GIs found pictures
of the leading citizens,
hands high in the air,
parading, showing the
Nazi salute, so they
pulled out the pictures
and hung all of them
on a big bulletin board
in the public square
with a sign that read,
in German:
There are no Nazis in Wörgl.

◆

Now the inmates
told me they
used to be
awakened at
three or four
in the morning
every day, and
marched to
the factories
near Munich
where they were
being worked.
The people of
Munich claim
that they never
knew. But that
isn't true.
They saw them
being marched
back and forth
every day.

*A*t this theater in Munich,
where the sixteen- seventeen-
eighteen-year-old boys, for
barter, would try to get our
cigarettes so that they could
exist, buy food, I took great
relish in taking a couple
of puffs, putting the butt on
the ground, rubbing it out so
they couldn't scrape it up.

◆

You've got a bunch of soldiers
standing around somebody's house with guns,
telling this family they have to get out,
so they leave, the wheelbarrow full of
belongings, and we move in: we
look for guns, we look for souvenirs,
smoked meat, food. We look for wine,
beer cached in the chimney, or the
attic. We know where it is. When
they come back there'll be cigarette
burns in the chairs and when they
complain we'll tell about Buchenwald.
We'll tell them:
You're lucky we didn't kill you.

*S*ix demitasse cups and six
saucers from the house
we'd taken over—I thought
they'd be a memento of
Germany. I thought my wife
would like them. Or the set
of silverware, a swastika,
the German eagle on the top
of the spoons. I took them
from the house. But the
longer I saw them, the less
I wanted the connection.
I didn't keep them.

◆

There's no conversation
when you're pointing a gun
at a German soldier's head.
You're not listening to
him, not asking him anything.
You're telling him: *Get up
on the hood of the jeep,* and
you're whipping him around
town, doing sixty, him trying
not to fall off. The only
thing he'd say, if he'd say
anything at all was:
I'm not guilty.

*T*he German army
was set free,
told to go home.
So they walked.
A thousand miles
home. And they
looked sad,
innocent, boys
swept up in war.

◆

*A*m I to judge
more severely
a man who was
a Luftwaffe pilot
than a good
friend who dropped
bombs on Dresden?
I mean, what's
the difference?

*W*hen I talked to
the Army chaplain,
I asked him if what
we saw in Germany
could happen in
America and he said,
No. He swore that
it couldn't. Then
we heard that
Hiroshima had been
blown to hell.
We all cheered.
The war was over.
We didn't care.

AFTER THE WAR

*O*ne guy
on the ship
on the way
home, he
went stark
raving mad.
I don't know
which of
the camps
he'd seen.

I'm being asked to relive
what I really have buried.
I don't thrive on it. If
I dwell on it, it bothers
me, like surgery you want
to forget about.

*E*verything that happened, happened
in a way by accident.
We weren't really briefed.
Suddenly the chaos, people
in the streets, rummaging garbage
for food, hovering around wherever
we had our mess kits.
I wasn't prepared for that.
I knew there were camps.
I was aware. I'd read a few things.
I enlisted because I was aware,
it wasn't just that I wanted to go
and kill people.

*E*ven though I was scared
and even though I was in
danger, I wasn't suffering.
I was secure within the
context of war. I cried.
I couldn't understand. But
it's not my story. It's
the story of those people.
I can't tell it. It's not
my story.

*A*fter the war, I
talked to my wife
about the camps.
But not explicitly.
No details. It's
hard to talk about,
and people don't
want to listen.
Once, I went to
a VFW club and
a couple of guys
were talking about
one of the camps.
I was listening
to them. But this
old guy told them
to stop. He didn't
want to hear.

◆

When I first came
home, I had to
sleep with a light.
My wife will
testify to this.
I used to see a
person, a faceless
soldier. It was
just a skeleton
in a helmet.

*I*n a nuclear war,
it'll be quick.
There won't be any
bands playing. None
of us will be in
the orchestra that
conducts us to the
crematorium.
It'll just be one
conflagration —
one gigantic oven.

◆

The enemy firing
at a soldier is
firing at an
impersonal target.
They don't know
who he is and he
doesn't know who
they are. After
the war I met
an awful lot of
German men, decent
men, nice men, who
a year earlier
would have shot me.

*M*y father came from
Poland. All the people
there were anti-Semites.
My father used to say,
*There's no such thing as
a good goy,* and I'd get
angry with him. This was
America. But when I
came to Dachau and saw
what the *goyim* had done
to Jews, I began to think
that my father was right.

◆

I've sold cars
for the past
twenty years
and anybody
who'd come in
with a German
accent, I had
no use for.
None whatsoever.
A nation that
allowed this
to happen
would allow
it to happen
again.

*S*ome of my best friends
are Jewish: my
coach, a person
I always liked and
respected; Charlie
Rappaport who made
a swimmer out of me;
Elain Kurlway, who
I went through
high school with;
Howard Freedman—
good friends of mine.
I don't look on them
as Jews. They're
just good friends
of mine. I didn't
think of them as
Jews before the war
and I didn't think
of them as Jews
when I came back.

✦

1.

This little car
came out of Dachau.
I picked it up
in the street.
Some child had
brought it. My
wife has painted
it black. She
painted the little
wheels red. I did
not see any children
in Dachau — alive.

2.

We always have
a Christmas tree
in our house. And
underneath the tree
we always have a
garden. We always
have skiers, farm
animals, a little
village and that
car from Dachau.
It's our family's
tradition.

I have a flag that flew
in Dachau. It flew in
Nuremberg. It flew in
Munich. It flew in all
the spots that I was in.
My wife sent the flag
to me. I felt that if
we took a place we should
say *here we are* so the
world would know that it
was America that came to
Dachau.

◆

At the University Theatre
in Harvard Square, I went
to see *The True Glory* and
I was still in uniform.
When they showed the films
of Dachau, the woman who sat
beside me said, *That's a lie.*
I was rugged in those days.
I just couldn't take it.
I said, *Lady, I've been there.*
I have seen this. This is real.
I still smell the stench.
And I said it loud and all
the people heard.

THE VETERANS

All of the poems in this book are derived from interviews with the following:

CASSIUS B. BARNES, Corporal, 9th Army, 395th Fighter Squadron, who carried the camera for Margaret Bourke White into Buchenwald

RABBI ELI BOHNEN, Major, Chaplain, 42nd Rainbow Division, Dachau

JOHN EDWARD CARPILIO, Technician 4th Grade, 1st Allied Airborne, 54th Signal Battalion, Company B, Ludwigslust

CHARLOTTE CHANEY, Second Lieutenant, R.N., 127th Evacuation Hospital, Dachau

JOHN A. CONNORS, P.F.C., First Infantry, 11th Armored Division, Mauthausen

JOHN C. COUGHLIN, 2nd Lieutenant, 1477th Engineers, Ludwigslust

ALLEN CRAMER, P.F.C., 21st Armored Infantry, 11th Armored Division, Gusen

JAMES CREASMAN, Technician 3rd Grade, 42nd Rainbow Division, Dachau

WALTER J. FELLENZ, Lieutenant Colonel Commanding, 42nd Infantry Division, 222nd Infantry, Dachau

EDWARD V. FITZGERALD, Staff Sergeant, 157th Infantry Regiment, 45th Division, Dachau

NATHAN FUTTERMAN, Corporal, 8th Infantry, 445th Anti-Aircraft Battalion, Wobbelin

PAUL KEVIN GALLANT, Corporal, 71st Artillery Division, 3rd Army, Dachau

WILLIAM GARDNER, Captain, 975th Field Artillery Battalion, Dachau

159

ALAN GOLUB, 1st Lieutenant, Fighter Pilot, 67th Tactical Reconnaissance Group, 109th T.R. Squadron, Buchenwald

ARTHUR HEIFITZ, Major, 87th Infantry Division, Ohrdruf

ELI HEIMBERG, Technician 5th Grade, Chaplain's Assistant, 42nd Rainbow Division, Dachau

GEORGE KAISER, Sergeant, 20th Armored Division, 8th Armored Military Battalion, Dachau

CARLETON B. LUND, Staff Sergeant, 179th Infantry, 45th Division, Dachau

DAVID MALACHOWSKY, Staff Sergeant, 7th Corps, 104th Infantry Division, 309th Medical Battalion, Company D, Nordhausen

COLONEL CURTIS MITCHELL, Special Messenger for the War Department, Belsen

JEROME PASTENE, Technician 5th Grade, 12th Replacement Depot, Dachau

KERMIT PRANSKY, P.F.C., Tank Destroyer Outfit, 87th Division, Buchenwald

WARREN PRIEST, Surgical Technician, 120th Evacuation Hospital, Buchenwald

TIMOTHY J. REIDY, Staff Sergeant, 249th Bombardment Group, Heavy Aircraft, Belsen

RALPH TALANIAN, P.F.C., 71st Infantry Division, Echelon Headquarters, Gunskirchen Lager

ROBERT TAYLOR, 1st Lieutenant, 605th Tank Destroyer Battalion, 101st Field Artillery, Ludwigslust

ROBERT TIGHE, Corporal, 4th Armored Division, 51st Armored Infantry, Buchenwald

160

HENRY TOOMAGIAN, Technician 3rd Grade, 970th Engineers, 7th Army, Dachau

SEYMOUR YESNER, P.F.C., 5th Ranger Battalion, Buchenwald

CHRISTOPHER ZERVOS, P.F.C., 157th Regiment, 45th Rainbow Division, Dachau